PRAISE FOR JOHN PURSLEY III

"Pursley's sense of abiding formal control allows for such a smart sense of play, for such quick veerings of heart, and for utterly clear renderings of ineffable states of being."

Lia Purpura
Writer in Residence, Loyola University Maryland
Author, *On Looking: Essays*
Finalist, National Book Critics' Circle Award

"Pursley is a poet who thinks about transience. His poems are successful because he understands the absolute dependence between the dying moments relationship to the lifetime and the dying moments relationship to the form of the poem."

James Owens
Author, *An Hour is the Doorway* and
Frost Lights a Thin Flame

Supposing, for Instance, Here in the Space-Time Continuum

Supposing

FOR INSTANCE,

HERE IN THE
SPACE-TIME CONTINUUM

John Pursley III

APPRENTICE HOUSE
BALTIMORE, MD

Grateful acknowledgement is made to the editors
of the following journals in which several poems
in this collection have previously appeared:

88: a Journal of Contemporary Poetry: "If You Have Ghosts"
AGNI: "[I Keep Imagining Mahler (In the Photographs . . .]," "In the Air"
Aura Literary Review: "Everything in Changes," "On Relationships"
Backwards City Review: "The Gourds We Picked Upon"
Center: "Untitled Interior"
Chelsea: "What Fourteenth-Century Chinese Hermit
Ch'ing-Hung (Stonehouse) Might Have Said
to the Twenty-first Century in Light of Recent Events,"
"Lex Non Scripta"
Cold Mountain Review: "Ghazal"
The Country Dog Review: "After the Gold Rush"
Crying Sky: "Black Cloud," "Commensuration & Slow Dissolve"
Diode: "Figure for the Lessons of Water,"
"Approaching Literature of the 21st Century"
H_NGM_N: "Skyland Boulevard" (2)
New Hampshire Review: "Of Unbroken Harmony"
Lumina: "Returning from an Exile; Suddenly Rain"
Parthenon West Review: "Spell for Shades of Migration"
Pebble Lake Review: "An Original Sound"
Red Mountain Review: "A Short History of Architecture"
Runes: "A Long Shadow of Clouds,"
"Supposing, for Instance, Here in the Space-Time Continuum"
Six Little Things: "Skyland Boulevard" (1)

ISBN: 978-1-934074-38-1

Apprentice House
Communication Department
Loyola University Maryland
4501 N. Charles Street
Baltimore, MD 21210
www.ApprenticeHouse.com

Acknowledgements

I wish to thank *Center* for nominating "Untitled Interior" for a
Pushcart Prize and *AGNI* for nominating [I Keep Imagining
Mahler (In the Photographs . . .]" for Best New Poets 2008. I
also wish to thank *Verse Daily* for featuring "Untitled Interior"
on their website.

I am grateful to the support and kindness of many teachers
and friends. First and foremost, I must thank Robin Behn, Joel
Brouwer, Bill Knott, Donald Revell, Bruce Smith, and Karen
Volkman, the best mentors I could hope to have. I would also
like to extend thanks to Sarah Blackman for all of her help and
support, Abraham Smith, David Welch, Tim Croft, and Flannery
Higgins Raney, as well as my sisters, friends, and especially my
mother and father.

CONTENTS

UNTITLED INTERIOR

The grapefruit tree has died.
But it isn't that.

Each leaf falling—stem-end
Over blossom. Pad

To slats. Cheap pine.
Pianissimo. As if there isn't air.

Isn't water. Lightly, lightly.
Enough to say this.

This. *This*, the one dead note.
Held like a stuck key.

SUPPOSING, FOR INSTANCE,
HERE IN THE
SPACE-TIME CONTINUUM

A LONG SHADOW OF CLOUDS

> —*to life's empty vanishing, a monument stands,*
Li Po reflects on Hsien Mountain,
> *long since blotted out beneath green moss*—

Later he would be exiled from Hsün-yang.
A sickly, wandering refugee,
                somewhat delusional, they say.
                The night all around him

As much as he was or could be—
            a part of this life. Legend has it

He fell drunk into a river & drowned
Trying to embrace the moon—

            but we lose our shadows
                    as we gain our form
            —and certainly, he must have jumped.

Quartz entombed in black siliceous stone—
Its radiance reflected
                and absorbed. We find ourselves here.

Among crystalline sediment, back-lit we see the sun.
How it patterns the silhouette of this body
                            and the next—

The apparition of landscape & cadmium horizon,

the long shadow of clouds.

Ten thousand years of standing still, & still
        pushing closer—farther away.

————————

Evening sun-shaft through backyard sycamores—

Alive with comings & goings. A noisy wood thrush
Gathers twigs in dead leaves

        beneath gnarled blackberry bushes, shuffling his feet.
The penumbral hawk circles the sky. The cars upon the freeway.

I am turning over the earth again,
                        to protect what little I can
    of time & space & the efforts of spring.

        Today, I am less sure
            and more convinced—

The ground is solid. Three-fourths flint & rock.
I pick up a shovel-split stone—all mineral & light—
            and brush it with my hands.

        A woodpecker somewhere
                        in the trees keeps time.
            A long shadow of clouds
                where we expire with the sun.

————————

How soon we forget failure—
Repeat ourselves & scribble out names in notebooks.
Here is an arm. A leg & hands fragmented.

      Bone-splinter, touchstone streaked,
This is a rock. This is the field
         where we leave our skins again.

The parchment coils under a sundry of smattered stone.
There is a rhythm in the wind. A single hawk upon the sky.

      Somewhere is an edge of light.
      Somewhere our revenants are passing—

COMMENSURATION & SLOW DISSOLVE

When the walls would turn, we'd disappear, we'd disappear she said, though she had meant to reappear as something else, something different than what they were, & she slept with the usual concerns—his arm, cocked-crooked beneath the soft friction of her breasts. The headlight's loom—left to right—quick along the walls, their irregular rhythms, circular, confused: He imagined they were lost teens who'd pulled into the cul-de-sac to turn around, & fell to sleep thinking of their bodies. And when he awoke, she was missing an arm, & he was surprised, but more so that he hadn't noticed before. It was a Saturday, & she was fixing toast. She rose to meet him, took him round the shoulder, said "good morning," & he smiled. Her thin frame, a near seamless hull of hips & thighs: She seemed smaller, more beautiful than ever, & he took her there, in the easement between the couch & kitchen. But in the shower, he could think only of her awkwardness, the unequivocal way she moved her body, like the blurred delineation of fire; & still, there was a certain newfound sense of excitement about her, unfamiliar, yet foundational, as mortar on brick, or the window, through which he watched her slow waltz across the yard *was she leaving?* settle among the puckered gladiolus, her body bent to bring them in. He dressed quickly & ran to her & she reached for him like a child, or a body on a battlefield, straining at last to lift itself, or be lifted, but without the contempt, without the raw emotion of it. He pulled her to him, & the grass snapped back into shapely spears absorbing the small indentation of her body, & he both loved & hated her, in her slow decline, her disfiguring *was she shrinking?* into the distance: It was easier this way, her smallness, almost painless, to watch her lethargic dissolve. She seemed helpless, & yet calm, so at ease with it all. And he laid her upon a pillow, & she looked at him as she hadn't in years, as

if he'd done some great deed, as if her prince had come to kneel
before her bed. An ample sorrow for her, for himself, swept him,
a feeling he couldn't quite contain or wrap his arms around. He
went to the kitchen for water, for air, for the screws that tightened
in his chest, & when he returned it was if she had diminished
to a viceroy of herself, nothing he could do now, nothing to be
said to set things right, nothing rational, except to internalize; she
was beautiful & he smiled, cupped her in the small of his hand,
mouthed meaningless words, & as if the world couldn't end, or
quite possibly exist, he swallowed her like a tiny tule boat, as if to
preserve, or to release, something of her, to feel her soft dissolve
into the tongue, her sweetness, her commensurate leaving.

GHAZAL

Legend has it Han-Shan would talk to trees of Cold Mountain,
His poems, like his body, would find surface in shadow.

Before they cut into him, the doctor offered a Sharpie,
Said: "X the right knee"—every closet has its share of shadows.

Each morning a child & his father drop lines to fish for trout.
Each morning a child & his father lose themselves in shadow.

Redbuds flower, open up afternoons when the sun is right.
Across the pallid lawn, their long shadows flow into shadows.

Blue: Azure: Indigo: Prussian: Sapphire: Turquoise: Cobalt
Skies like a watershed—the drift of clouds, the lazuline shadows.

Woody Guthrie writes *This Machine Kills Fascists* on his guitar &
Returns to the Brooklyn-State Hospital—the old shadows.

The drop of rock, the echo & ripple, the one hand clapping,
The other to write it down: pebbles shelving in the shadows.

She picked the orange from the blue bowl & turned it in her hands,
Her eyes fixed upon the skyline, the tamarack's heavy shadows.

[I Keep Imagining Mahler
(In the Photographs ...]

I keep imagining Mahler (in the photographs my mind constructs
To make meaning) holding his daughter in a field of blue poppies

And standing so still, his shadow *melded* with hers, seems to carry
More weight than his actual figure—which is slight & impossible

To read as anything more than a study in blue: a blue, impossible
Even in Vienna, or south, along the shores of the Adriatic: a blue

Which rivals *only* Mahler, so alone with this child, no one bothers
To raise her head, which has slid from the shoulders to the purse

Of his arm, or nearly, so tired is she? And Mahler, whose shadow
Falls along the Danube . . . whose shadow dies along the Danube,

Whose shadow wavers when I am not looking . . . whose shadow
Rises, like a hawk, having outgrown its own heart, whose shadow

Falters once, then twice—& has the good sense to fail . . . Mahler
Who holds the oldest of his children, Marie, above a field of blue,

Mahler who is humming bars from *Frère Jacques* & something else
I cannot place, something darker, brutal, barely audible to the ear.

———————

As a child, sometimes it is difficult *to know* the measure of a voice,
To hear & not hear, the wind rushing through wheat, the timbres

Of a father's voice calling up the stairs . . . the sovereign, spectral,
Undefined. I think of my mother's voice, *& then* of Marie, listless

Against her father's chest—& already dying . . . a bacterium toxin
Corporaled through the blood, like potassium cyanide, the tangible

Sounds of rainwater, turning out of gutters—flooding the streets,
The neighboring yards & parks, still heavy with winter. In Vienna

Among men whose teeth yellowed, *like antique ivory*, like lightning-
Struck oak after a summer of rain—among men, who kowtowed

To her father, cantering before him, like appaloosas turned loose
On two toppled apple-carts, abandoned in the city—among men,

Who would seek to do him harm . . . *Putzi*, little Marie, struggling
To stay afloat above an ocean of blue poppies, struggling to hear,

To know, each note, as it passes from her father's lips—struggling
To breathe within the animal of her body—*which has failed*, which

Continues failing, &, *with each failing*, keeps falling, *faster*, farther in.

SKYLAND BOULEVARD

Slip inside this house   the road inside the road

Where the burdock & weevil   seem a chattering

Of what is really here   a dead ground, swollen

With the late sounds of war   the religious right

The bridges to Babylon   Tuscumbia & so many

Red lights set like Stations of the Cross   a holy

Victual like "Holy smokes, Batman!!!"   how far

We are from heaven   it's a manner of measure

A mere chattel of time, to us   what difference?

Put a good foot forward   & the highway opens

Up a little   slip inside this house, this road this

Tiptoed through tulips   & tell me what you see

FIGURE FOR THE LESSONS OF WATER

I was young   taught the children how to swim   their mothers

Came   I made them air to breathe   to see the children made

To breathe   some water lopped about the eardrum   the chest

Cavity caved into itself   the pressure of that water   & the ear's

Drum taught them how to breathe   made them   how to swim

———————

I was young   transfixed by water   a container of water painted

To look bluer than it was   by air & the mothers there   before

And after lessons   the knobby knees of children   the bleached

Sprawl of children   against the concrete decks   where breathe

Meant breathe & the eardrums droned   to crawl   meant swim

———————

I was young   figuring for the body's mass   some percentage of

Which is the air   supposing for water   another 55-60 percent

Roughly   figuring for variations & the throat   how it breathes

Roughly in the ear   swims in the ear   the air I made it breathe

From their mother's mouths   a kickboard back   to/from here

I was young   timing their lungs capacity to hold   to breathe

The bodies of their mothers   in the bleachers   their throats

Parched with lack of air   parched with the swim   the how to

Of breathe & breathe   capacity for body's mass   made them

To swim   figure for the lessons of water   how one breathes

In the Air

And in the spring—
When the disk-plow turned this land,
Back into fields, & pheasants

Coughed their hoarse songs of morning,
We watched our breaths dip & waver
With the fog, through pin oak & pine,

Hovering like the questions of rain.

And you said you'd seen a field mouse
Lie dead, *"The hens pecked out his eyes*
And left the wind to 'buck & wing'."

> *Around & around, Old Joe Clark*
> *Around & around we go—*

And down along the riverbank,
Where the bargemen load & reload
Commerce to flat-bottom freighters,

Dead fish, bloated, oscillating in watersheds,
Gathered flocks of perennial scavengers

Pulsing in slow drag with the sky.

And today we watched & waited
As if something were to happen—

You crouched low to the ground,

Kicking footholds in the earth,
And I scattered seed for black birds;

The rush and whir of highway songs,
Silent ghost lights through the fog.

A Short History of Architecture

The office building where my father worked
        Day, *& night*, stands high above the square
                Like a protractor's rough edge
Worn smooth though generations of use
        And misuse, rounds Dakota and Main sprawled
                Like tributaries in its wake. Hardly visible
Now, the vestiges of the old grocery store
        And the insurance office haunt the living
                Space of the upper floors, the apartments
And the old dance hall in blankets of dust,
        Quiet, untouched, as if expecting something
                Or someone to find among dilapidated walls
The familiar standards of a different day,
        Familiar. As a child, I frequented those
                High ceilings with my mother & father
Who explained how architecture unfolded,
        Itself a story, describing the less-elaborate
                Intricacies of each eave as the more modern
Late-Victorian, the red brick as characteristic
        Queen Anne, while my mother & I
                Uncovered old ads on rusty signs & waxed
Cardboard cutouts—*Remember a Loaf*
        Of Butternut Bread, & *Sweetheart Flour,*
                Exceptionally Good!, Dr. Pepper 10-2-4—
From among the rows of Sunkist crates,
        The old newspapers & campaign signs in stacks
                Along the walls & piled in the dusty bottoms
Of porcelain claw-foot tubs. But it wasn't until
        I was older that I really took to the place,
                Visiting alone, crawling the steep stairs

In the middle of the night, the only light,

       Billowing up, through immense key-hole

              Windows, from the streetlights of the square.

Half-lit, I'd stumble through the wreckage,

       Of boxes & old vegetable racks, carving a path,

              That soon became familiar, to the dance hall,

Where I'd wait to hear voices, the stories

       Of the place, scaring myself to scare myself.

              None ever came, only footfalls

All my own & the echoes of my voice

       Talking to no one in particular, a call

              Without response. Still, I remember

The bricks, cool & moist with perspiration,

       And when the evenings were warm, I'd climb

              Onto the rooftop, high above the pigeons'

Nests & the lights of the square, look

       Out at the grid of houses up & down

              The roads. Sometimes I'd dance along

The cupola, knowing no one could see

       My inane assembly of silly dances, or just lie

              On my back, & stare at the sky, drifting

From red to purple, & wait for stars to blossom.

After the Gold Rush

1.

When I was born
They said I should

Have a sister

Fifteen seconds later
I had a sister

They laid us out
Like corn

Pulled & stretched
Our arms

Said this is yours

This is yours

2.

Hum of halogen
Click luminary

So many halos

So many hollows
Hidden

The eye
And the spleen

Like large
Carnivorous birds

3.

Late night
Gentle whir of wipers

Always the turning
And returning

Always the gentle
Fracture of the streetlights

The quick click of a door
The slow walk of steps

Echoing along hallways

4.

Return to the house
The childhood home

Impossible

To begin

At the beginning

Unfortunate sad hours

Sad clocks tick ticking
My mother

Always older
Says something

Of the Shermans
Their field's

Return to native

Prairie grass
Says

The grocery doesn't
Carry tahini

Perhaps we should make
The potatoes wedges

IF YOU HAVE GHOSTS

The dark is enough: the smallness of morning
Before the first light slides, carefully
Along the banister, where
My whole life, over polished wood & the imperfections
Of wood, I have run my hands,
Pressed lightly on the same steps, the same door
Where I know my parents are sleeping . . .

We are never alone—though, to understand it
For the first time must come as a surprise for a child,
The way a window, opening
Or suddenly snapped shut, can suggest
Change in the weather, an approaching storm
Or the stillness following—the quiet
Murmur of earth, lights that never go out.

The difference is in being small & understanding
One's smallness. *Every angel is terrifying*—
Let them sleep where they may. Turn & go back.
Across the hall to your room, lie down,
Naked, beside your own body & comfort
In its breathing. There are still a few good hours
Between morning & much work to do.

SUPPOSING, FOR INSTANCE,
HERE IN THE SPACE-TIME CONTINUUM

Maybe—if we lie here a little longer, letting our toes
        Touch in the late fashion of preadolescent bluebirds
Or lovers, squaring their bodies to whatever melody
        The water makes, gurgling against rocks, a few twigs

And the broken beer bottle that, given its proximity
        To the bank, & the fair-to-moderate clip the current
Cuts around the bend, scoring the glass to an almost
        Delicate green, could *almost* be beautiful—supposing

For instance, time carries all things towards a point
        Of departure, & the old man feeding carrier pigeons
Will one day die, the last bits of a sandwich, glazing
        His upper lip & the lapels of his suit, tired & serving

No practical purpose after fifty-six years of working
        Numbers into columns, into vacations & sports cars
He'd never indulged in, selling even the old Chrysler
        He cut to the curb each morning, on the hill outside

The bakery, where he'd sometimes stop—for coffee,
        Or a muffin—& later, letting the tires roll a few feet
Before popping the clutch & heading towards home,
        After the death of the dancer, he'd refused to marry,

Though they'd shared a house together once, before
        The cancer crept back into her breast, & his pension
Proved too little to support them both—suggesting,
        Perhaps to some extent, mutual separation, distance,

The cold hard facts of life, the way an old man looks
          After his car has been bought & sold & towed away,
The lines on his face growing hard—then blemishing
          To a softness like leaves, like fire . . . that misfortune

A person must feel, watching his whole house go up
          In flames, *& realizing*—standing under the streetlight
Where the snow seems to fall the hardest & the cars,
          Slowing to watch as fire climbs the walls & windows,

The asphalt shingles of the roof, seem almost frozen
          For a moment, like statuaries, against so much snow
—*how* inconsequential it all must seem to the firemen,
          Working overtime & on call & this far into the night,

And how, when the first floor gives, the whole thing
          Will come crashing down . . . not in tears, or blurred
By fire—but in the sudden shudder of pigeon wings,
          Taking flight, lifting their big, dumb bodies in the air,

And then settling back down—strutting the tall grass
          In praise of their surroundings: the old man standing
Like an oracle, among birds—his arms, outstretched
          In a gesture so simple, we might mistake the dancing

He does, for an attempt at flight—a lover's humility
          Dissipating, *in* time . . . into ash, into bottles, broken
Against the crags in the creek bank; the picnic tables
          No one uses, standing alone—*so* solitary, so sublime

In the weight of their construction, we could believe
        Almost anything: the shy vernacular of late romance,
Where we all might live in a world of simple pleasure
        Or, eventually, supersede time—&, almost be happy.

SKYLAND BOULEVARD

And I am in love with the Chardonnay   the hard spackled lights,

The all you can eat buffet   fat with fritters   little craw, crayfish,

Lobster, spice an atrium of reunion this brutal closet, this mini-

Malled arch of earth   this expenditure   thoroughfare to Jesus,

Jay-Z & we're in it   over our heads with the late Jimmie Rodgers

It's peach pickin' time in the upper atmosphere   the American

Thrift   repeating itself in tintinnabulation reciprocity & rebound

Relationships   doubling for the real thing   like the seltzer pop

Of bubbly   food & fast   like the giddy-up & go of graveyards

One headlight, hubcap, hills in every direction   little clay runnels

Clandestine with shopping   with Lowe's, Payless   *why pay at all?*

Even the theaters begin to cloud the stars with Right Turns Only

Headstones you can mow over   just enough gas for getting there

RETURNING FROM AN EXILE;
SUDDENLY RAIN

Above the schoolhouse, tulip trees
               Divide the upper pastures—where
The arroyo ran white with water

     Cut by an angular swath of light &
               The divot-hunks of horses' hooves
Dried along the bank. Stubborn-

     Like, they'd blossom there—green,
               Then white, all that orange igniting
About the middle like a conduit

     Belled to amplify—or *to entreat?*—
               The wind, the way our ears opened
To the sounds of rain, doubling

     Down the commonweals of water
               That banked along the ankle-bones
Of the cormorants fishing trout

     And tiny sea bass by the bucketful.
               But when we cross the upper ridge
To see the city where they lived

     Like kings & princes, paupers—all,
               I can't see sign of a single elk—still
We stall along the bank & scrim

The water with our hands, hopeful
                        Just to touch a fish as it swims past
And watch the patter of the rain,

                Pounding out its despondent tune,
                        Touching the fish as they swim past,
As they swim past & past & past.

SPELL FOR SHADES OF MIGRATION

Take these rocks, this gravity
Made flesh. Let them lodge
Into the stomach: *the darker the berry,*

The sweeter the juice. Of night,
Know only enough
To know what can be tucked away

Or peeled apart. Know talons,
The hollows of eyes, sockets.
Know the rise of barns, crossbeams

And eaves, the construction
Of this life. Glide of wind
In blossom of day lilies. Open

Out into air. Settle the houses
In slopes of green,
In city swells & wiregrass gardens.

Yellow the light, touched down
In pulse upon water—or just rising off.
Let this loosing be the eyes,

The shadows be emptying.

BLACK CLOUD

There is a black cloud settling over the in-
    Town houses & the firemen pearl-waxing
The ladder truck—their cautionary yellow
    Suspenders wet with water *or* perspiration
It is hard to tell—I think—without saying

Anything—though the eyes give me away,
    And already you've discerned my appetite
For the loneliness of others, & the elderly-
    Older man, wearing his yellow suspenders
Down around his ass, like the paratrooper

Trainees at Lackland, has begun rolling up
    The door to the garage, & I am visualizing
His wife, at home, standing over the stove
    Or straightening the drapes by a television
That hardly works, a tiny table set for two,

Twenty-some-odd minutes still left on the
    Meatloaf. We should take a vacation while
We still have time, you suggest, you know
    Before the summer's over, but I'm several
Blocks down the street, following the boy

Walking his dog, turning into the familiar
    Cut grass of home, & the hydrangeas look
Lovely—& besides, what with work & all,
    And the cats, *how could we leave?* It's almost
Lunchtime; it's beginning to look like rain.

Lex Non Scripta

Tuesday morning—skies like a watershed
Above & behind
                    the line of trees in the backyard
Not clouds exactly. Not the strict auras—

Weeks upon weeks of waiting
                              and finally rain
Last night & the night before last—
But not now, not here
                        in the backyard
Of my own first home, watching the contractor
And his tired steps—

Settle back into the house
                          to paint
What's left of the living room.
Everyone is busy with something.

It's November & the cicadas have gone.
The leaves have lost their crispness.

Even the hushed whole of the traffic cutting
                              the corner to Hargrove
Stops—starts & drives on through

As if there is some place to be—
As if anything is open.

Approaching Literature
of the 21st Century

Where are the clouds? She pointed up & just under.

His truck, rusting in the yard beneath an apple tree.

Under the milkweeds, more grass, a bunch of blue.

Three, four more hours, the dog would come back.

Unbroken, the woman shrugged another marriage.

On the rear of the wagon: a cantaloupe, a blue tick.

How understanding, she said, but would not return.

AN APPROXIMATION OF STARS

beyond these, windows   light   of sun   or later
    the conditional   moon

                              our kitchen

the little silence, here

                fallen through   this & this

here

                & *here*, in this

    the house

                we thought possible   an earring

(forgotten &/or) lost   found, again
                snaggled through
    a sweater   doubtless   something of Chistmas

all this   what it is

                it is

to say

the smallest gesture of   *this*, this moment
          lifted up   impossibly lifted

                                        held

to let the in-light   out

                the approximation of stars

like moon-flies   dust is   all we have

What Fourteenth-Century Chinese Hermit Ch'ing-Hung (Stonehouse) Might Have Said to the Twenty-first Century in Light of Recent Events

Each morning—undercut,
Erosive, the sun

Comes quick

Above the mountains,
Looks out

Over the inlet's round lobes,

Patterns itself
Upon the pavement,

Upon parking meters,
The prominence of

Rectangular building,

Hunkers down
Upon house

And home, says
It's time, it's time,

Just before the wind
Rolls out & gathers clouds

Meandering between
The shipyards & the harbor

And blows them
Like sails, silent

Along the streets.

EVERYTHING IN CHANGES

So much sorting over, so much undone—
Ten-thousand years of penciling skylines & still
                    I know nothing of the horizon;
            the way water aligns the surface of itself
                    before it climbs to crest—

The black shape of ocean water,
                                rising into itself, falling
Into itself, curls into something of darkness—
                    and everything in changes.

                I lay down sketches
To watch the way water meets the sky disappearing
        into nothingness—how it gathers, reappearing as conditional
                            star-fleck & moon-swallow.
A little darkness,
                here. A patch of light glitters & goes under,
            and nothing, again, matters.

Today, I skip stones out over the water & watch them
                        vanish in a flux of long drawls,
As delicate ends of seltzer-surf, spangle up
                        in the shallows at my feet—

                A scraggly, neighborhood
                cocker spaniel approaching from out of the
                darkness,
        lifting his nose as if he were the pinnacle
Of some forgotten mooring, he has no intention of chasing.
I scratch his chin & call him *good*—

Good, I say, as if I hadn't heard myself correctly. *Good*,
in the same way I greet a morning
                        cup of coffee or the passing cars
        on their way to work.

On Relationships

When we've reduced them to what we are
And only the ribbed skeletons
                                against the skyline
Remain, shadowing us as we shadow each other

Everything changes. The shapeliness of the mangroves,
Cypress & sweet gum disappears—
                                reappearing
Awkward as elbows & the knobby parts of knees.

The moon & its flatness lifts
                        what's left of landscape
And scatters it as it likes—

The doldrums of the dory's unhinged end
Unfold themselves
                        splayed out under starclusters.
Things are not always what they seem,
                        you say.

No one remembers where we've been
                                or why we've gone.
Still, when darkness falls, & the center shifts
They recognize our leaving.

SPELL FOR LONG MORNINGS

Hardened acidic the orange
Peels like husked old shells
Of snails or roses. Exhale these.

Mornings of summer immersed,
Shed the wings slowly—
First secondary,
Then primary. Flight.

Forgive the dog his incessant prattle.
The neighbor's leafless scatter.

Green the plants of those living,
And the having lived—
Throw them out. Hum the bees
In quiver of rosebud.

Know the millipede & the rabbit,
The ants & their hills.
The strange spice of oranges
Drying, know this.

Lay down.
This body, a floor for limitless day.

"Of Unbroken Harmony"

If tonight, *again*, I dream of you, Thoreau—
If tonight I dream of you & rain—if rain should choose
To hammer out its shape upon the water

In the likeness of itself, or the likeness
To which it too conforms—

Forms only a kind of prolonged static, holding—
The sky in the homogeneous frequency
Of white noise—this tiny boat between us now,

Still taking water, tacking N/NW
In another form of silence . . .

If tonight, our voice lacks strength enough to speak,
And only motion forms from our lips,
Strike a paddle against the boat, strike the paddle

And we'll elicit the sound of birds, the titmouse
And squirrel, the woodchuck, now heavy with winter—

Strike your paddle as if to speak . . . speak now
Dear silence, dear me . . . speak now
In the likeness of your voice, or the likeness

To which it conforms . . . say something, anything,
And I will begin bailing the water.

AN ORIGINAL SOUND
—for Galway Kinnell

There is comfort in the boot, well-worn,
Comfort in the echo of each
                                   step, lightly
Exacting the next,
Exacting the ones which came before—

The earned space (These repetitions, of
Which are ours?),
                         the *scritch scritch scritch*
Of snow among trees—that is Kinnell's
That Silent Evening . . . where we walk out

Together, the little of it we think, or not.
In this life,
               only
That the world remain, this
Harrowing speck—tabular? Repetitious?

That with each step fallen, the branch be
Not broken,
                   the scrub oaks & pitch pine,
The quiet pleasantries of snow,
That the grass, be it common shrubbery,

Or of some other, be not too much bent
As the wind passes over it,
                                   that old bones
Callous in winter, that these boots be not
Splintered too far from the heel.

The Gourds We Picked Upon

fire the radish   the kiln   in red wine & rosewater

hollow the gourds   we picked   upon the ground

can you not hear   the birds   warbling their throats

between two words   worlds like plums   crashing

behind barns   decorated like houses   or children

by children   emaciated swallows   the loosed tooth

of a rake   the tines   till death do us   a warbling

About the Poet

John Pursley III is the author of two other chapbooks: *A Conventional Weather* (New Michigan Press, 2007) and *When, by the Titanic* (Portlandia Press, 2006). Recently, he was co-winner of the Sarah Lawrence College Campbell Corner Poetry Prize and winner of the Fugue Poetry Prize. *If You Have Ghosts*, his first book, was the Editor's Prize Selection for the Zone 3 Poetry Prize and will be published in 2010. Pursley earned his M.F.A. in Creative Writing (Poetry) at the University of Alabama. He teaches writing and literature at Clemson University.

Apprentice House Annual Chapbook Competition

The poetry chapbook contest is for poets previously unpublished in book form (previous chapbooks are okay). Winner receives $250 prize and 25 copies. Look for contest classified ad announcmenet in the Janaury/February issue of *Poets & Writers* magazine. Deadline is mid-March. Rules and prizes subject to change. For the latest submission guidelines, please go to www.ApprenticeHouse.com, call 410.617.5265, or e-mail info@apprenticehouse.com.

Judges for the Second Annual Chapbook Competition

Ned Balbo, poet, Apprentice House editorial board member, and Affiliate Associate Professor in the Writing Department at Loyola University Maryland.

Lia Purpura, Loyola University Writer in Residence and Author of *On Looking*, a Finalist for the National Book Critics' Circle Award.

THE FUTURE OF PUBLISHING...TODAY!

Apprentice House is the country's only campus-based, student-staffed book publishing company. Directed by professors and industry professionals, it is a nonprofit activity of the Communication Department at Loyola University Maryland.

Using state-of-the-art technology and an experiential learning model of education, Apprentice House publishes books in untraditional ways. This dual responsibility as publishers and educators creates an unprecedented collaborative environment among faculty and students, while teaching tomorrow's editors, designers, and marketers.

Outside of class, progress on book projects is carried forth by the AH Book Publishing Club, a co-curricular campus organization supported by Loyola University's Office of Student Activities.

Student Project Team for *Supposing, for Instance, Here in the Space-Time Continuum*: Ali Sampson, '09.

Eclectic and provocative, Apprentice House titles intend to entertain as well as spark dialogue on a variety of topics. To learn more about Apprentice House books or to obtain submission guidelines, please visit www.ApprenticeHouse.com.

Apprentice House
Communication Department
Loyola University Maryland
4501 N. Charles Street
Baltimore, MD 21210
Ph: 410-617-5265
info@apprenticehouse.com

www.ingramcontent.com/pod-product-compliance
Lightning Source LLC
Chambersburg PA
CBHW071428040426
42445CB00012BA/1290